JOHN DALY

CW00496153

The Life and Career of John Daly - A Comprehensive Exploration of the Golf Legend's Rise to Fame, Battle with Addiction, and Moments of Triumph.

Kimberly Howerton

COPYRIGHT

All rights reserved. No part of this book may be reproduced, entered into a retrieval system, or communicated in any form or by any means, electronic, mechanical, photocopying, recording, or otherwise, except brief excerpts contained in critical reviews and other noncommercial uses permitted by copyright.

COPYRIGHT © Kimberly Howerton 2024

TABLE OF CONTENTS

INTRODUCTION

John Daly, a name synonymous with both remarkable golf prowess and tumultuous personal battles, is a figure whose life and career have captivated audiences around the globe. Daly was born on April 28, 1966, in Carmichael, California, and his rise from humble beginnings to becoming one of the most recognizable faces in professional golf is nothing short of remarkable.

Daly's introduction to the sport came at an early age when his father introduced him to golf as a way to escape the troubles of their tumultuous family life. Despite lacking the traditional country club upbringing that many professional golfers receive, Daly quickly demonstrated an innate talent for the game. His powerful swing and fearless approach to the course distinguished him from his peers, foreshadowing the unconventional path his career would take. His golfing talent blossomed early, leading him to the University of Arkansas on scholarship. However, his rebellious spirit clashed with expectations, and he turned professional in 1987 without completing his degree.

Daly made his professional debut at the 1991 PGA Championship, which was held at Crooked Stick Golf Club in Indiana. As an unknown rookie, Daly was not even guaranteed a spot in the tournament but gained entry as the ninth alternate. Seizing the opportunity with both hands, Daly not only made the cut but stunned the world by winning the championship with his long drives and unorthodox playing style. This victory, despite all odds, propelled him into the spotlight and earned him the nickname "Long John."

Despite his meteoric rise to fame, Daly's career has been fraught with challenges both on and off the golf course. His battles with alcoholism, gambling addiction, and turbulent personal relationships have been well documented, frequently overshadowing his professional accomplishments. Daly's candor about his demons and his unwavering resilience in the face of adversity have endeared him to fans who see him as a flawed but relatable figure.

Throughout his career, Daly has amassed an impressive list of accomplishments, including two major championship titles—the aforementioned 1991 PGA Championship and the 1995 Open Championship at St. Andrews. However, his success has been marred by inconsistency and controversy, including PGA Tour suspensions and weight and fitness issues.

Despite the controversy, Daly continued to demonstrate flashes of brilliance on the course. He added four more PGA Tour victories to his tally, including the 2004 Buick Invitational, which ended a five-year drought and served as a testament to his resilience.

But the off-course struggles persisted. Daly continued to battle his demons, undergoing multiple stints in rehabilitation. Nonetheless, his charisma and self-deprecating humor kept his fan base loyal.

Through it all, Daly remained a polarizing figure. Some praised his honesty and rebellious spirit, while others criticized his self-destructive tendencies. Regardless of perspective, there's no denying his impact on the game. He brought excitement and unpredictability to a sport often seen as staid, attracting new fans with his relatable struggles and unlikely triumphs.

Today, at 57, Daly remains a polarizing figure, a golfer whose immense talent was often overshadowed by personal challenges. His story, however, goes beyond wins and losses. It's a story about second chances, redemption, and the enduring strength of the human spirit.

CHAPTER ONE

Early Life and Influences

John Daly's story is one of defying odds and carving his own path. From a transient childhood to becoming a major champion, his formative years shaped the distinct personality and golfing talent we know today. Born in 1966 in Carmichael, California, Daly's childhood was marked by frequent moves due to his father's construction work. This instilled in him a sense of adaptability and resilience, qualities that would help him on the golf course and in life. At the age of four, the family relocated to Dardanelle, Arkansas, where young John discovered his passion for golf on the local public course.

Daly's father, Jim, was an avid golfer who introduced John to the game at a young age. Jim instilled in him a passion for the sport and a strong work ethic. However, John also credits his mother, Lou, for her unwavering support and encouragement, even when things got tough. Daly's natural ability was undeniable. His long-hitting and effortless power drew attention. However, amidst his brilliance, turbulent undercurrents emerged. He struggled in school, clashed with authority, and showed early signs of alcohol dependence. Despite his talent, his unconventional approach and disciplinary issues raise doubts about his future in golf.

As Dally progressed through his teenage years, his talent continued to blossom, earning him recognition at the regional and national levels. His outstanding performances in amateur competitions drew attention from college recruiters and golfing associations, paving the way for the next chapter in his career.

Daly's talent was evident early on. He won local tournaments at 13 and earned a scholarship to the University of Arkansas. A half-scholarship to the University of Arkansas offered an opportunity for structure and mentorship. While his talent shone on the golf course, his issues with alcohol and attendance persisted, resulting in a strained relationship with coaches. Despite not graduating, Daly improved his skills and gained valuable competitive experience.

Daly turned professional in 1987, embarking on a journey marked by both successes and setbacks. He quickly found success on regional tours, his power and flair attracting attention. However, personal demons continued to haunt him. Gambling, alcoholism, and suspensions marred his early career, raising concerns about his ability to maintain success.

Daly's Path to Professional Golf

John Daly's journey to professional golf was marked by determination, perseverance, and unwavering dedication to his craft. From his humble beginnings as a young golfer with aspirations of competing at the highest levels to his eventual rise to prominence on the professional circuit, Dally's story exemplifies the triumph of talent and tenacity over adversity.

Daly's journey from amateur to professional golf began with a series of pivotal moments and formative experiences that shaped his future path in the sport. As a standout player in junior and amateur competitions, he caught the attention of scouts and recruiters who recognized his potential for greatness. His success in the early stages of his career gave him the confidence and momentum he needed to take the next step towards professional golf.

John Daly's amateur career was marked by numerous notable accomplishments and successes, laying the groundwork for his eventual rise to prominence in the world of professional golf. Dally's amateur golf accomplishments ranged from impressive junior tournament victories to standout performances on collegiate circuits, demonstrating his exceptional talent, dedication, and competitive spirit.

One of Daly's amateur career highlights came during his high school years when he established himself as a dominant force in local and regional junior tournaments. His natural talent and competitive drive distinguished him from his peers, earning him recognition as one of the best young golfers in his area. Dally's success in the junior circuit gave him valuable experience and confidence as he pursued his passion for golf at the collegiate level.

The 1983 Missouri State Amateur Championship was a significant milestone in John Daly's early golfing career, serving as a springboard for his rise to prominence in the world of golf. This prestigious event, held at various golf courses throughout Missouri, drew top amateur golfers from across the state, all competing for the coveted title.

John Daly was only 17 years old when he won the championship in 1983, but he demonstrated skill and poise far beyond his years. Despite facing stiff competition from more experienced players, Daly displayed his natural talent and competitive spirit throughout the tournament, demonstrating an exceptional ability to navigate difficult courses and handle the pressure of high-stakes competition.

Winning the Missouri State Amateur Championship at such a young age was a significant accomplishment for Daly, proving his potential as a future golf star. The victory drew attention from golf fans and experts alike, who recognized Daly's talent and predicted a bright future for the young golfer.

In 1984, John Daly won the Arkansas State Amateur Championship, adding to his impressive amateur golf record. This victory followed his win in the Missouri State Amateur Championship the previous year, solidifying his regional dominance and confirming his status as one of the sport's most promising young talents.

Daly's victory at the 1984 Arkansas State Amateur Championship demonstrated his exceptional skill, mental fortitude, and competitive spirit. Competing against a field of seasoned amateurs on difficult courses across Arkansas, Daly once again demonstrated his ability to rise to the occasion and perform at his peak when it counted the most.

The 1986 U.S. Open: John Daly's Glimpse into the Majors

John Daly's rise to professional golf stardom was not a straight line. It was fraught with detours, challenges, and flashes of brilliance, one of which was his participation in the 1986 US Open. This prestigious major championship served as a critical stepping stone, demonstrating his talent and reigniting his desire to play in the Major Leagues.

As a 19-year-old amateur, Daly wasn't expected to make much of a splash at the notoriously challenging Shinnecock Hills course. Nonetheless, he defied expectations by qualifying for a local sectional tournament, demonstrating his raw talent and long-hitting ability. This was no small feat, given that the US Open attracts the world's best professional golfers.

Daly's first-round performance wasn't what he or his supporters hoped for. A rough 88 (+8) put him well behind the pace and appeared to end any hopes of making the cut. However, the second round revealed flashes of brilliance that would become his signature. He carded a much-improved 76 (+4), demonstrating his ability to recover from setbacks and fight under pressure.

The 1986 U.S. Open was a turning point for Daly. He tasted the big-league atmosphere, felt the thrill of competing alongside legends, and saw the potential in his own talent. This glimpse fueled his ambition and sparked a strong desire to become a professional golfer.

The tournament also held personal significance. Jeff Medlin, Daly's caddie during the event, became a mentor and friend, eventually caddying for him during his historic PGA Championship victory in 1991.

Daly's experience at the 1986 U.S. Open was more than just making the cut or winning the tournament. It was a turning point moment that propelled him into professional golf, showcasing his talent and sparking his ambition. It was a glimpse into the future, a taste of the success that lay ahead, and a testament to the raw talent that would define his unconventional and captivating career.

The media coverage of his performance catapulted Daly into the public eye, making him a well-known figure even before turning professional. This newfound recognition presented both opportunities and challenges, impacting his personal life and interactions. The taste of major championship competitions fueled Daly's desire to pursue a professional career. He saw the US Open as a glimpse into his future, and it inspired him to take the next step.

The challenges of Shinnecock Hills helped him hone his skills and competitive edge. He learned how to handle pressure, strategize in difficult situations, and showcase his unique strengths on stage. The media attention generated by the US Open led to sponsorships and opportunities, allowing him to launch his professional career.

Daly's decision to turn professional in 1987, just one year after the U.S. Open, was heavily influenced by the tournament's impact. It acted as a catalyst, propelling him toward his goal of competing at the highest level. He'd tasted the thrill, seen his own potential, and received the recognition that cemented his desire to make golf a career.

Daly's Gritty Journey: Navigating Minor Tours with Wins and Demons

John Daly's rise to professional golf stardom was not a fairytale journey. Following a promising amateur career, he embarked on minor tours, battling financial difficulties, personal demons, and relentless pressure. This crucible, however, forged his resilience, honed his skills, and instilled the "never say die" mindset that would define him.

The minor tours were a far cry from the prestigious U.S. Open. Long drives, spartan facilities, and meager purses became Daly's reality. He frequently slept in his car, worked multiple jobs to make ends meet, and struggled with the emotional impact of constant competition and pressure to succeed.

Daly, already prone to impulsive decisions, grappled with personal demons during this period. His battles with alcohol and gambling addiction added another layer of complexity to his struggles. While these issues hampered his consistency, they also fueled his desire to prove himself and get out of his situation.

Despite the challenges, Daly's talent shone through. He won tournaments on several minor tours, including the 1988 Ben Hogan Utah Classic and the 1989 Hooters Tour Championship. These victories provided not only financial relief but also crucial confidence boosts, proving he could compete and win.

The minor tours taught Daly a hard lesson, but he emerged as a more resilient and resourceful player. He learned to adapt to new courses and conditions, control his emotions under pressure, and never give up on himself. This "never say die" attitude, combined with his natural talent, would become a defining feature of his professional career. The minor tours were difficult, but they were also an important part of Daly's story. They shaped his personality, honed his abilities, and laid the groundwork for his improbable rise to fame.

Daly's Cinderella Story: The 1991 PGA Championship

John Daly's 1991 PGA Championship victory wasn't just a win; it was a seismic shift in the golfing landscape. As a ninth alternate, a virtual unknown with a checkered past, Daly defied all odds to win the prestigious title, catapulting himself to instant fame and etching his name in golf history.

Daly's path to the tournament was far from ordinary. He secured his spot just days before the event, thanks to other players' withdrawals. Arriving with little practice and low expectations, he embodied the true spirit of an underdog. His unconventional attire - loud shirts, baggy pants, and a mullet - set him apart from the polished professionals.

Daly defied expectations from the very first tee shot. His booming drives and fearless approach challenged the notoriously difficult course while captivating audiences. He faced seasoned veterans such as Bruce Lietzke and Chip Beck, displaying steel nerves and incredible shot-making ability under pressure. Daly's underdog status fueled his determination. He started strong, with powerful drives and aggressive play that captivated audiences. Despite a mid-tournament slump, he showed remarkable resilience by coming back with clutch birdies and eagles.

The last round was a rollercoaster. Daly made crucial birdies and gutsy pars despite facing challenges on each hole. The final stretch was filled with thrilling drama. A double bogey on 17 threatened to derail his lead, but a crucial birdie on 18 sealed his improbable victory.

Daly's three-stroke victory sent shockwaves throughout the golf world. The unknown ninth alternate had won one of the sport's biggest stages, proving that talent and determination could overcome any obstacle. His emotional celebration, which included throwing his winning driver into the crowd, strengthened his bond with fans and solidified his image as a relatable, everyman hero.

The 1991 PGA Championship was not just about the trophy. It was a gateway to fame and fortune. Daly quickly became a household name, landing lucrative endorsements and invitations to prestigious tournaments. The victory provided financial stability and allowed him to pursue a life he had only imagined.

Daly's victory was not without its consequences. The sudden fame and pressure brought personal issues to the forefront. His struggles with addiction and personal demons became public fodder, resulting in a complex narrative alongside his golfing accomplishments.

Despite the challenges, the 1991 PGA Championship remains the turning point in Daly's career. It demonstrated his raw talent, unwavering determination, and ability to work under pressure. It was a victory not only for him but also for the spirit of defying expectations and believing in the impossible.

CHAPTER TWO

Beyond the PGA: Exploring John Daly's Championship Pedigree

While John Daly's 1991 PGA Championship victory is unquestionably his most famous accomplishment, his competitive spirit and talent were evident in several other notable tournaments and championships throughout his career.

1990 AECI Charity Classic:

John Daly's victory at the 1990 AECI Charity Classic on the South African Sunshine Tour was a critical early step in his professional career. Daly was able to showcase his talents on an international stage while also gaining valuable experience against a diverse field of competitors.

At just 24 years old, Daly was a relative unknown, having turned professional only three years prior. He competed against seasoned competitors on the Sunshine Tour, which was a testing ground for aspiring golfers at the time. His victory highlighted his raw talent, powerful driving ability, and surprisingly well-rounded game.

Daly entered the final round tied for the lead with David Feherty, a respected Irish golfer. The final day was a fierce battle, with both players exchanging birdies and bogeys. Daly eventually won by one stroke, holing a clutch par putt on the final hole in dramatic fashion.

The AECI Charity Classic victory was Daly's first as a professional golfer, indicating his potential for success at the sport's highest levels. The win not only boosted Daly's confidence but also gave him much-needed momentum as he began his professional career.

Daly's victory in the AECI Charity Classic provided him with valuable exposure to the global golfing community. Competing in the South African Sunshine Tour.

Competing on the South African Sunshine Tour exposed Daly to a variety of playing conditions, courses, and competition styles, which helped him broaden his perspective and hone his skills as a professional golfer.

1991 PGA Championship:

John Daly's victory in the 1991 PGA Championship remains one of golf's most remarkable Cinderella stories. As the ninth alternate and a virtual unknown, Daly seized the opportunity to compete in the tournament and stunned the golfing world by winning the championship. His incredible distance off the tee, combined with his fearless approach to the game, propelled him to victory, making him the most unlikely of major champions.

1992 B.C. Open:

John Daly's 1991 PGA Championship victory may have propelled him to stardom, but his first PGA Tour victory at the 1992 B.C. Open at Broome County Club was extremely significant, serving as validation of his talent and potential.

The B.C. Open was not a major championship, but it did feature a challenging course with undulating greens and narrow fairways. It was an opportunity for Daly to demonstrate that he could win on more difficult layouts, rather than just wide-open courses where his length could dominate.

The 1992 British Columbia Open was held at the En-Joie Golf Club in Endicott, New York. The course, known for its tight fairways and demanding greens, provided a different challenge than the wide-open spaces that Daly had thrived in at the 1991 PGA Championship. This victory showcased his versatility and ability to adapt to diverse layouts.

Daly wasn't the only star competing for the title. Tom Kite, an experienced professional known for his precision and strategic play, pushed Daly throughout the tournament. Their contrasting styles made the final round a thrilling battle of power and experience.

Daly started the tournament strong, firing a 68 in the first round. Despite facing challenges throughout, his long drives and clutch putting kept him in contention. In the final round, he faced an experienced opponent in Tom Kite, a 16-time PGA Tour winner known for his precise ball striking and strategic play. The final round became a thrilling battle between Daly's strength and Kite's experience. Daly birdied the 16th hole to take the lead, but Kite birdied the 17th to tie. Both players reached the par-4 18th in two, setting up a dramatic finish. Daly started the final round two strokes behind Kite. Despite a rocky start that included a bogey on the first hole, he rallied with birdies on the 3rd and 4th. He continued to trade blows with Kite, displaying composure under pressure and sinking clutch putts on key holes.

The turning point occurred on the 17th hole, a par three. Daly's daring tee shot landed inches from the hole, allowing for a birdie putt. He drained it, eliciting a roar from the crowd and giving himself a one-stroke lead. Kite faltered on the final hole, leaving Daly with a two-stroke lead and the opportunity to seal the victory. With a par on the 18th, Daly secured his first PGA Tour win, raising his arms in triumph. The emotion was palpable, as this victory came just months after his stunning PGA Championship victory. It cemented his status as a rising star while also validating his unconventional style.

This win held multiple layers of significance; Following his unexpected PGA Championship victory, some questioned whether Daly's success was a fluke. This victory on a different course against established players such as Kite silenced doubters and proved that his talent was not a one-off. It marked the start of his PGA Tour career, proving his ability to compete and win against the best in the world. The victory also showcased the effectiveness of his aggressive "grip it and rip it" approach, inspiring a new generation of golfers.

1994 BellSouth Classic:

John Daly's 1994 BellSouth Classic victory was more than just a trophy; it demonstrated his versatility and ability to conquer a variety of courses. The Walt Disney World Resort course, with its shorter yardage and strategically placed water hazards, seemed ideal for Daly's attacking style. While his long driving was always useful, this tournament required precise shotmaking and a strong short game, both of which he had been steadily improving.

Daly did not simply dominate the course. He showed remarkable control over his driving, hitting fairways with impressive consistency. His short game was sharp, sinking key putts and navigating the challenging greens with confidence. This balanced approach, combining power and finesse, was critical to his success.

The tournament was a nail-biter, with Daly up against defending champion Nolan Henke and Brian Henninger. The final round featured several lead changes, keeping the crowd on edge. Daly's poise under pressure and ability to execute under intense competition was critical to his success.

In the final round, Daly was tied for first place with three other players. He birdied the par-5 14th to take sole possession of first place, but a bogey on the 16th forced him into a one-stroke tie with Henninger. However, Daly responded with a clutch birdie putt on the 17th, putting him one shot ahead of Henninger heading into the final hole. A par on the 18th hole sealed the victory, sending the Florida crowd into a frenzy.

1995 Open Championship:

John Daly's victory at The Open Championship in 1995 captivated the golf world and is still remembered as one of the sport's most iconic moments. This championship, held at the historic Old Course at St. Andrews, also known as the "Home of Golf," is the oldest of golf's four major championships, with a long history and prestige.

Daly arrived in St Andrews under intense pressure. Having won the PGA Championship four years prior, he craved another major title but faced scrutiny for his personal struggles and unconventional style. The historic

Old Course, known for its unpredictable winds and quirky bounces, added an extra layer of challenges.

Daly's victory in the 1995 Open Championship was nothing short of remarkable. Daly had already established himself as a fan favorite, known for his incredible distance off the tee and fearless approach to the game. However, his victory at St. Andrews would cement his reputation as one of the game's most electrifying players. Daly's tournament took place in two halves. He started strong, shooting a 66 in the first round showcasing his powerful driving and putting. However, the second and third rounds proved more challenging, with fluctuating scores and missed opportunities.

Daly's fortitude shone through on the challenging Old Course. Despite setbacks, he remained focused and adjusted his strategy, relying on his instincts for the links and scrambling effectively. He famously holed a 40-foot putt on the 18th hole of the third round to keep his title hopes   alive.

The tournament's climax occurred during the final round when Daly found himself in a thrilling duel with Italian golfer Costantino Rocca. As the tension rose and the pressure increased, Daly demonstrated steel nerves, producing clutch shots and critical putts to maintain his lead on the leaderboard.

However, it was the dramatic playoff on the 18th hole that cemented Daly's place in golf history. After Rocca made a miraculous chip shot for birdie to force the playoff, Daly responded with a composed and confident display of golfing prowess. His final approach shot to the green, followed by a routine two-putt, sealed the victory and sparked scenes of jubilation among galleries and fans around the world.

Daly's 1995 Open Championship victory was monumental: it cemented his place in golf history as a two-time major champion, silenced critics, and demonstrated his ability to perform under pressure. Winning on arguably the most iconic golf course in history gave him immense prestige and demonstrated his adaptability to different playing conditions.

2001 BMW International Open:

The 2001 BMW International Open victory marked a significant milestone in John Daly's golfing career, showcasing his global appeal and success beyond the PGA Tour. This prestigious European Tour event drew top players from all over the world and gave Daly the opportunity to compete on a global stage.

Daly's victory at the 2001 BMW International Open demonstrated his versatility as a golfer and his ability to adapt to a variety of playing conditions and environments. Despite competing against seasoned European Tour professionals on unfamiliar courses, Daly rose to the occasion with his trademark flair and tenacity, thrilling fans with powerful drives and precise shot-making.

Daly's victory was fueled by a combination of his signature power and impressive precision. He unleashed his powerful drives on the long par 4s and 5s while demonstrating remarkable iron and short-game accuracy on the tighter holes. This balanced approach proved extremely effective on the difficult Eichenried layout.

Daly did not just win; he dominated. He led by four strokes after the first round, shot a course-record 62 in the third round, and won by six strokes. This demonstration of power and precision wowed European audiences unfamiliar with his style.

The tournament wasn't a one-man show. Daly had stiff competition from established European players such as David Howell and Phillip Price. The final round was a thrilling battle, with Daly edging his opponents by one stroke. His dramatic birdie putt on the 18th hole sealed the victory and sent the crowd wild.

His victory cemented his status as a global golfing star, demonstrating his ability to win on a variety of circuits while captivating international audiences. It was his first major European Tour title, which opened doors to new opportunities and established a strong fan base in Europe. His presence and thrilling victory raised the profile of the BMW International Open, bringing more attention and sponsorship to the event.

2004 Buick Invitational:

In 2004, John Daly's victory at the Buick Invitational marked another significant milestone in his career, demonstrating his ability to overcome adversity and prevail against a competitive field of fellow professionals. The Buick Invitational, held at the prestigious Torrey Pines Golf Course in San Diego, California, was a PGA Tour event that drew top players from all over the world.

Daly had to overcome numerous obstacles on his way to victory. He had struggled with gambling addiction, alcoholism, and personal issues, all of which had an impact on both his professional and personal life. He had dropped significantly in the world rankings and had not won a PGA Tour event since 1995.

Torrey Pines held special significance for Daly. He had nearly won the U.S. Open there in 2000, finishing second in a heart-wrenching defeat. Returning in 2004 brought both excitement and pressure, testing his mental fortitude and desire to overcome past demons.

Throughout the tournament, Daly displayed flashes of brilliance and inspired play, demonstrating the talent and skill that had won him over fans around the world. His powerful drives off the tee, combined with precise iron shots and deft touch on the greens, catapulted him to the top of the leaderboard and put him in contention for the title.

Daly started strong, but the tournament remained a tight battle with Luke Donald and Chris Riley. Entering the final hole tied, Daly's drive found a deep bunker. Faced with tremendous pressure, he hit a miraculous 100-foot bunker shot, leaving him inches from the hole for a tap-in birdie. Donald and Riley missed their birdie putts, giving Daly an emotional victory.

Daly's victory at the 2004 Buick Invitational was not only a demonstration of his golfing talent and skill, but also a celebration of his resilience and perseverance in the face of adversity. It was a victory that strongly resonated with fans and fellow competitors alike, serving as a reminder of sports' transformative power to inspire and uplift in the face of adversity.

The victory propelled Daly back into the spotlight. He enjoyed initial success, finishing in the top 10 eight times over the next two seasons, including a second-place finish at the 2004 Buick Open. This newfound confidence enabled him to compete in a variety of events and reestablish his competitive rhythm. However, the road wasn't paved with consistent triumphs. Injuries, including back and knee issues, began to impede his performance. Coupled with occasional off-course issues, his return faced inconsistency. While flashes of brilliance persisted, he struggled to match the brilliance of his peak years. Despite regaining some status, Daly still struggled financially. The prize money was insufficient to cover his debts, putting pressure on his performance. Moreover, media scrutiny continued, often focusing on his personal struggles rather than his golfing achievements.

2017 PGA Tour Champions Toshiba Classic:

John Daly's victory at the 2017 Toshiba Classic (now known as the Hoag Classic) demonstrated his enduring competitive spirit and ability to adapt to a new chapter in his golf career.

The Toshiba Classic, held at Newport Beach Country Club, marked Daly's second year competing on the PGA Tour Champions circuit for players 50 and older. While his power driving remained an asset, he needed to adapt his strategy to shorter courses and a new competitive environment.

Daly teamed up with veteran player Steve Jones for the event, utilizing a "best ball" format where the lower score of each player on each hole counts towards the team score. This format allowed Daly to concentrate on his signature long drives, while Jones' experience and precise short game provided valuable support.

After four rounds of consistent play, Daly and Jones were tied for the lead with two other teams. A dramatic playoff ensued, with Daly and Jones demonstrating their distinct abilities. Ultimately, they prevailed on the third playoff hole, securing their first-ever victory as a team.

Major Milestones: Unveiling John Daly's Journey Through the Grand Slams

John Daly's golf career has been a rollercoaster ride, with dramatic victories, heartbreaking near-misses, and moments of controversy. Throughout his career, the four major championships - the Masters, the U.S. Open, the Open Championship, and the PGA Championship - have served as crucial testing grounds, revealing his immense talent, undeniable challenges, and lasting impact.

The Masters: Daly's performances at Augusta National Golf Club, the home of The Masters, have been a mix of high and low. His best finish came in 1993 when he tied for third, demonstrating his ability to compete on one of golf's most iconic stages. Daly's relationship with The Masters has been fraught with controversy, including a 1994 suspension from the tournament for failing to properly sign his scorecard. Despite the setbacks, Daly's performances at The Masters remain an important part of his legacy in the sport.

U.S. Open: Daly has had both success and disappointment with his performances in the U.S. Open. His breakthrough victory at the 1991 U.S. Open at Crooked Stick Golf Club is one of the most memorable events in golf history. As the ninth alternate, Daly stunned the world by winning the title, demonstrating his prodigious talent and fearless style of play. However, Daly's success at the U.S. Open has been overshadowed by missed opportunities and near misses in subsequent years, including several missed cuts and withdraws.

The Open Championship (British Open): The Open Championship has been a source of both triumph and frustration for Daly throughout his career. Daly's victory at the 1995 Open Championship at St. Andrews is regarded as one of the most memorable moments in tournament history, cementing his status as a major champion. However, Daly's subsequent Open Championship performances have been inconsistent, with flashes of brilliance punctuated by missed cuts and disappointing finishes.

PGA Championship: Daly has experienced both success and controversy at the PGA Championship over the years. His victory in the 1991 PGA Championship as a relatively unknown player remains one of the most unlikely victories in golf history. Daly's victory at Crooked Stick Golf Club demonstrated his incredible talent and resilience, propelling him to golf superstardom. However, Daly's association with the PGA Championship has been fraught with controversy, including several high-profile withdrawals and missed cuts in subsequent years.

John Daly's Legendary Driving Distance and its Impact

John Daly's booming drives have not only propelled him down fairways, but have also carved a unique path in golf history, forever associated with his nickname "Long John" and his reputation as one of the game's longest hitters.

Daly's swing was anything but textbook. His unconventional mechanics, including a wide stance, aggressive takeaway, and a "chicken wing" finish, challenged norms. Yet, his unorthodox approach generated incredible clubhead speed, consistently exceeding 120 mph and occasionally reaching speeds near 150 mph.

Daly's swing was a marvel of power and unconventionality. His wide stance, aggressive coil, and unconventional release produced tremendous clubhead speed, propelling the ball further than anyone else on tour. Unlike many golfers who rely on arm strength,

Daly's power came from his exceptional body rotation, which effectively transferred energy from his core to the clubhead.

Daly's length provided a distinct advantage on many courses, allowing him to reach par 5s in two and overpower doglegs, often putting him in prime scoring positions. His incredible distance terrified opponents and boosted his own confidence, especially in pressure situations. His booming drives, which frequently exceeded 350 yards, drew crowds who appreciated the excitement and raw power of his game.

Daly's success with his unconventional style challenged accepted beliefs about swing mechanics and inspired a generation of young golfers to try new approaches. His dominance in driving distance prompted other players and equipment manufacturers to prioritize distance gains, resulting in an increase in average driving distance across professional tours.

John Daly Biography

CHAPTER THREE

Personal Struggles and Controversies

John Daly's life has been marked by a series of personal struggles and controversies, which have frequently played out in public, influencing both his career and public image. Daly's journey has been marked by highs and lows, triumphs and setbacks, ranging from his well-documented struggles with addiction to his turbulent relationships and legal issues.

John Daly's Struggles with Alcohol and the Road to Recovery

John Daly's career has been marked by both incredible successes and heartbreaking struggles, with his battle with alcohol addiction playing a significant role in his story. John Daly's battle with alcohol addiction is a well-documented aspect of his life, one that has had significant impacts on both his career and personal life. Daly's struggle with alcoholism has been a recurring theme throughout his life, from publicized incidents to tumultuous relationships.

Daly's relationship with alcohol started at a young age, and he has openly discussed his early drinking and partying experiences. As he rose to prominence in the world of golf, Daly's lifestyle often mirrored the excesses of fame and fortune, resulting in frequent episodes of binge drinking and reckless behavior.

The impacts of Daly's alcohol addiction on his career were profound and far-reaching. Despite his undeniable talent and potential as a golfer, his struggles with addiction frequently overshadowed his successes on the course. Daly's erratic behavior, missed tournaments, and withdrawals due to alcohol-related issues became all too common, raising concerns about his dedication to the sport and ability to reach his full potential as a professional athlete.

In addition to the professional repercussions, Daly's alcohol addiction also took a toll on his personal life, contributing to strained relationships, failed marriages, and legal troubles. His tumultuous marriage to his third wife, Sherrie Miller, was marked by domestic violence, substance abuse, and public spats, culminating in a highly publicized divorce and custody battle. The addiction also had an impact on his physical health, causing weight fluctuations and other complications. It also led to suspensions from tours, affecting his ranking, earnings, and reputation.

Despite the challenges he has faced, Daly's journey towards recovery has been marked by moments of introspection, growth, and resilience. In recent years, he has been open about his struggles with addiction and the impact they have had on his life and career. Daly has sought treatment for his alcoholism and has taken steps to improve his mental health and wellbeing.

In addition, Daly has become an advocate for addiction recovery and mental health awareness, using his platform to share his story and support others facing similar challenges. He has openly discussed the importance of seeking help, connecting with support networks, and committing to a sober lifestyle.

Suspension and Reinstatement: Unveiling the Story Behind John Daly's PGA Tour Controversies

John Daly's career has been marred by controversies, including PGA Tour suspensions, which have had far-reaching consequences for both his professional and personal life. These suspensions were the result of a variety of incidents, including behavioral issues, disciplinary infractions, and addiction struggles, and they tested Daly's resilience and determination to compete again.

Daly's first suspension from the PGA Tour occurred in 1992, when he walked off the course during the Kapalua International tournament in Hawaii. This incident, which Daly later blamed on frustration with his performance and personal issues, led to a six-month suspension from the tour. Despite the setback, Daly returned to the competition determined to prove himself and reclaim his place as one of golf's elite players.

In 1993, Daly was suspended for violating Tour rules by picking up his ball mid-round in an unofficial tournament. He received a fine and probation upon reinstatement. The event in question was a pro-am charity tournament in Florida, not an official PGA Tour event. Daly reportedly picked up his ball mid-round at a Pro-Am event preceding the official FedEx St. Jude Classic due to frustration with his performance. This violated Rule 30-3 of the PGA Tour's Code of Conduct, which prohibits players from withdrawing from unofficial competition without a valid reason. The exact reasons for Daly's withdrawal remain unknown, with some citing frustration with his game and others hinting at potential sponsor conflicts. Regardless of the motive, the violation resulted in disciplinary action. The Tour investigated the incident and issued a two-week suspension, which was later reduced to one week, as well as a fine and probation. This suspension occurred just as Daly was establishing himself on the Tour, following his impressive performance at the 1991 PGA Championship. It was a setback, disrupting his playing schedule and potentially jeopardizing his early momentum.

Following an altercation with a spectator in 1994, Daly was suspended for five months for conduct unbecoming of a professional golfer. While accounts vary, it's widely reported that Daly exchanged heated words with a spectator who heckled him during the tournament. Some versions mention Daly throwing a piece of sod in the spectator's direction, although this remains disputed. Prior to issuing the suspension, the Tour conducted a thorough investigation, interviewing witnesses and gathering evidence. Following the incident, Daly publicly apologized for his actions, recognizing his error and expressing regret. The suspension had a significant impact on Daly's career, disrupting his playing schedule and affecting his ranking and earnings. This incident further fueled negative perceptions of Daly's behavior and character, adding to the challenges he faced in regaining public trust. Daly later apologized for his actions and recognized the importance of learning from his mistakes and dealing with challenging circumstances with greater composure.

In 2008 He earned a six-month suspension for conduct detrimental to the Tour after spending a night in jail for disorderly conduct. Daly was arrested in North Carolina in July 2008 for disorderly conduct and public intoxication, and he spent one night in jail. While the specific details of the incident remain disputed, his actions violated the PGA Tour's Code of Conduct, specifically the rule regarding "conduct detrimental to the best interests of the Tour." As a result of this incident, the PGA Tour suspended Daly for six months, citing his behavior as detrimental to the tour's image. This suspension added to Daly's career-long history of disciplinary actions and controversies.

John Daly's Off-Course Controversies

John Daly's career has been defined not only by incredible golfing achievements but also by a series of off-course controversies that have sparked widespread public attention and debate.

Public Intoxication and Disorderly Conduct: Throughout his career, he has been arrested multiple times for alcohol-related incidents, which has harmed his public image and resulted in suspensions and fines.

Gambling Addiction: His well-documented struggles with gambling addiction have played an important role in some off-course controversies, emphasizing the difficulties of recovery and responsible behavior.

Domestic Violence Allegations: Accusations of domestic violence have cast a shadow over his personal life, raising societal concerns and legal issues.

Breaking the Stigma: John Daly's Openness about Mental Health

John Daly's career has transcended the golf course, becoming a story of athletic prowess intertwined with personal struggles. His openness about his mental health struggles, particularly depression and addiction, has resonated with many people, raising awareness and providing valuable insights.

Daly has openly discussed his struggles with depression and anxiety since his early career, citing childhood experiences and the pressures of professional golf as potential contributing factors. He hasn't shied away from talking about his struggles with alcoholism, publicly entering and re-entering treatment programs, and acknowledging the difficulties of recovery. In 2007, Daly was diagnosed with bipolar disorder, which provided additional context and understanding for his mood swings and emotional volatility.

In a nutshell, John Daly's openness about his mental health struggles has been a powerful force for awareness and advocacy, helping to demystify discussions about mental illness and encouraging others to seek help and support. Daly's courage, vulnerability, and resilience have demonstrated that it is possible to overcome even the most difficult challenges and emerge stronger on the other side.

CHAPTER FOUR

Dally's Approach to Mental Toughness and Sports Psychology

John Daly's professional golf career has been a roller coaster of spectacular triumphs, dramatic comebacks, and personal challenges. While his unconventional style and outspoken personality have received a lot of attention, less is known about his unique approach to mental toughness and how it contributed to his success. John Daly's approach to mental toughness and sports psychology is a fascinating aspect of his career, with a distinct blend of natural talent, raw emotion, and unconventional techniques. Throughout his career, Daly has demonstrated the power and limitations of mental toughness in golf, providing insights into the complex interplay of mindset, emotion, and on-course performance.

Daly's career is frequently cited as a shining example of the value of mental toughness in golf. Despite his unconventional swing and approach to the game, Daly's raw talent and unwavering self-belief have propelled him to remarkable success on the course. His ability to maintain focus and composure under pressure, combined with his fearless attitude and aggressive style of play, has enabled him to overcome adversity and achieve success despite seemingly insurmountable odds.

One of the defining characteristics of Daly's approach to mental toughness is his struggle to manage his emotions on the course. Daly, known for his volatile temperament and fiery outbursts, has frequently struggled to cope with the mental demands of professional golf. His emotional highs and lows have served as both a source of strength and vulnerability, propelling him to victory on occasion but also resulting in costly mistakes and missed opportunities.

Despite his struggles with emotional control, Daly has shown remarkable resilience in the face of adversity. He has repeatedly overcome setbacks and challenges, refusing to allow his emotions to dictate his performance or define his career. Daly's ability to recover from disappointment and failure demonstrates his mental toughness and determination to succeed despite all odds.

Daly's career has been marked by ups and downs, and his approach to mental toughness has evolved as he has encountered new challenges and experiences. While he may have initially relied on his raw talent and bravado to navigate the mental demands of professional golf, Daly has also learned to adapt and refine his approach in response to changing circumstances and experience-based insights.

Daly's journey in golf has been marked by numerous difficulties and setbacks, but each of these experiences has provided valuable lessons in mental toughness and resilience. Whether overcoming personal challenges or encountering adversity on the course, Daly has learned to turn setbacks into opportunities for growth and self-improvement. His ability to recover from disappointment and failure demonstrates his mental strength and determination to succeed.

John Daly's Memorable and Controversial Quotes

John Daly's career would be incomplete without delving into his memorable and sometimes controversial quotes. His career has been defined not only by his powerful drives and electrifying victories, but also by his outspoken personality and memorable quotes. These sayings, which range from humorous quips to controversial statements, provide insight into his personality, humor, and, on occasion, the challenges he faced.

"Grip it and rip it!": This iconic phrase, which is frequently oversimplified, reflects Daly's aggressive style and confidence in his powerful driving. It could be

interpreted as encouraging risk-taking and trusting your instincts, but it also has the potential drawback of neglecting strategic finesse.

"It's nice to worry about playing golf and not all the other stuff.": This quote highlights the pressure and scrutiny Daly faced. It may appeal to anyone seeking relief from overwhelming stress, but it also raises concerns about potential avoidance mechanisms.

"Golfers are the dumbest athletes on the planet.": This provocative statement sparked debate. While it may reflect dissatisfaction with certain aspects of the golfing culture, it comes across as disrespectful to other athletes and risks perpetuating negative stereotypes.

"I am not here to win a popularity contest." "I am out here to win golf tournaments." Daly's spirit of competition and unwavering focus on winning is encapsulated in this quote. It reflects his no-nonsense approach to the game of golf and his willingness to put success ahead of public approval. While some may

consider Daly to be brash or abrasive, this quote demonstrates his dedication to excellence and willingness to go to any length to achieve his goals.

"I do not work out. If God wanted us to bend over, he'd put diamonds on the floor." This quote exemplifies Daly's aversion to traditional fitness routines and embrace of a relaxed lifestyle. It reflects his dislike for the rigors of physical training and his desire to live life on his own terms. While some have criticized Daly's lack of fitness, this quote exemplifies his irreverent sense of humor and willingness to challenge societal norms.

"Hit it hard." Go look for it. "Hit it hard again." This quotation perfectly captures Daly's direct style of golf, emphasizing strength and aggression. It reflects his belief in the value of distance off the tee as well as his willingness to take risks in order to achieve success. While Daly's aggressive style of play has produced some impressive results, it has also resulted in inconsistency and volatility on the course.

"I've always believed that the harder I practice, the luckier I get." This quote highlights Daly's commitment to hard work and his appreciation of diligence and preparation. It reflects his belief that success in golf is achieved through hard work and perseverance rather than talent or luck. While Daly may have received criticism for his off-course behavior, this quote demonstrates his dedication to his craft and desire to excel at the highest level.

"I'm a walking testament to the fact that golf is a mental game." This quote acknowledges Daly's mental health issues and the psychological challenges of professional golf. It reflects his understanding of the role of mindset and attitude in achieving success on the course. While Daly's mental toughness has been tested by adversity and personal demons, this quote exemplifies his resilience and determination to overcome challenges and achieve greatness.

CHAPTER FIVE

John Daly's Lasting Impact on the Game of Golf

John Daly's impact on professional golf extends far beyond his two major championship victories. His unconventional style, powerful drives, and outspoken personality have left a lasting impression on the sport, influencing everything from driving distance to fan engagement.

Longest Driver: Daly's prodigious length off the tee revolutionized the game of golf and forever changed the way players approached course strategy and equipment technology. Daly's booming drives, which routinely exceeded 300 yards, demonstrated the importance of power and athleticism in modern golf. His ability to overpower courses and reach par-5s in two shots challenged traditional course design concepts, forcing golf organizations to adapt by lengthening courses and implementing new equipment regulations.

Daly's reputation as the "Longest Driver in Golf" was more than just hype. He consistently pushed the boundaries of distance, inspiring a generation of golfers to put power first and redefining course design to accommodate longer shots. His influence went beyond individual technique, encouraging the development of equipment specifically designed for longer drives, thereby shaping the modern golf ball and driver landscape. Daly's success at distance challenged the notion that "long and wild" meant inconsistency, demonstrating that power could be used for strategic advantage and thrilling victories.

Fan Engagement: Daly, known for his everyman persona, colorful personality, and approachable demeanor, became a fan favorite and helped broaden golf's appeal to a larger audience. His relatable backstory, humble beginnings, and unfiltered authenticity resonated with fans from all walks of life, attracting new demographics to the sport and increasing interest in tournaments in which Daly competed. Daly's approachability and charisma won over golf fans worldwide, whether he was interacting with spectators, signing autographs, or engaging with the media.

Challenging Conventions: Throughout his career, Daly challenged conventional norms and expectations within the golfing world, often pushing back against traditional etiquette, dress codes, and behavioral standards. His irreverent attitude, flamboyant fashion choices, and occasional outbursts challenged the buttoned-up image of professional golf and added an element of unpredictability and excitement to the game. While Daly's behavior drew criticism at times, it also sparked important discussions about the changing nature of golf culture and the need for greater inclusivity and diversity in the sport.

Inspiring Future Generations: Daly's underdog story and unconventional path to success have inspired thousands of amateur and professional golfers to chase their dreams and overcome adversity. His fortitude in the face of personal adversity, setbacks, and public scrutiny serves as a source of inspiration and encouragement for aspiring golfers who may face similar obstacles on their own journey. Daly's willingness to share his experiences, both successes and failures, has helped to demystify the elite world of professional golf and make it more accessible to a wider audience.

Daly's impact on the game of golf extends beyond his statistical accomplishments and tournament victories, to his role as an entertainer and cultural icon. Whether he was hitting jaw-dropping drives, interacting with fans, or captivating audiences with his larger-than-life personality, Daly added excitement and spectacle to the sport that went beyond mere competition. His legacy in golf can be found not only in the record books, but also in the hearts and minds of those who were inspired by his fearless approach to the game.

Beyond the Fairway: Exploring John Daly's Diverse Business Ventures

John Daly's journey goes beyond the limits of professional golf. Aside from his electrifying drives and captivating victories, he has ventured into a variety of businesses, forging a path away from the greens.

Golf Course Design: John Daly has collaborated with golf course architects on designing golf courses, bringing his unique perspective as a professional golfer to the table. His involvement in course design allows him to help shape the game and leave a lasting impression on the golfing landscape. One notable project Daly has been involved in is the Lion's Paw Golf Links in Ocean Isle Beach, North Carolina. The course, designed by Daly and architect Tim Cate, features challenging holes and stunning views that demonstrate Daly's vision for the future of golf course design.

67

Apparel lines: Daly has also dabbled in the world of fashion with his apparel lines. He has launched several clothing lines, including Loudmouth Golf and John Daly Golf. These lines feature bold, colorful designs that appeal to golfers looking to make a statement on the course. While Daly's apparel lines have received attention for their distinct style and personality, their success has been mixed. However, Daly's brand recognition and larger-than-life personality have aided in driving sales and attracting customers to his clothing lines.

Daly's collaboration with Loudmouth Golf was a bold move, with vibrant and unconventional clothing designs that challenged traditional golf attire. The brand gained initial popularity, capitalizing on Daly's personality and the growing trend of embracing individuality on the course. However, its long-term success was limited by competition and shifting market preferences.

Music: In addition to his golf ventures, Daly has dabbled in the music industry, releasing several albums. He is a skilled guitarist and songwriter best known for his country and rockabilly-influenced music. Daly has performed at numerous music venues and events, demonstrating his musical abilities to audiences all over the world. While Daly's music career has not been as successful as his golf career, his passion for music and performing has allowed him to explore new creative outlets and connect with fans in new ways.

While he did not achieve mainstream commercial success, his music resonated with fans who appreciated his authenticity and willingness to experiment. His musical endeavors, though not a significant financial success, offered a glimpse into his personality and broadened the scope of his fan engagement beyond the traditional golfing audience.

70

John Daly Biography

CONCLUSION

John Daly's story is a tapestry woven with threads of triumph, turmoil, and triumph. From his electrifying drives that redefined distance to his personal struggles that touched millions, his story transcends golf history. He was more than just a player; he was a cultural phenomenon, a man who defied expectations, questioned norms, and won the hearts of fans all over the world.

This book has explored the complexities of his career, delving into his victories and struggles, his controversies and triumphs. We've seen his resilience in the face of personal challenges, his impact on driving distance and fan engagement, and his legacy as a champion who valued individuality and pushed boundaries.

Daly's career embodies the highs and lows of the human experience, from the exhilarating triumphs on the course to the deeply personal struggles off it. Despite each challenge and setback, Daly has remained steadfast in his resolve, facing adversity with courage and resilience.

Daly's legacy extends beyond trophies and accolades. He leaves behind a game forever changed, with longer courses and a more diverse fan base. He leaves behind a conversation about mental health, encouraging athletes and individuals alike to seek help and embrace vulnerability. He leaves behind the memory of a man who dared to be different, who swung for the fences even when the odds were stacked against him.

So, what will be John Daly's ultimate legacy? Perhaps there isn't a single definitive answer, but rather a constellation of possibilities. He is the epitome of raw talent, the champion who defied expectations, and the man who dared to bare his soul. He is a reminder that even the most imperfect journeys can leave an indelible mark, inspiring others to pursue their dreams and embrace their individuality.

Whether you remember him for his outrageous outfits, electrifying drives, or candid confessions, John Daly will leave an indelible impression. He was more than just a golfer; he was a story, a conversation, and a symbol of the human spirit's resilience and the ability to embrace the unexpected.

Printed in Great Britain
by Amazon

41590096R00046